11/10/8

To my
favori...

Happy b...

BLESSINGS
from the †
BATTLEFIELD

BLESSINGS
from the ✝
BATTLEFIELD
Edited by Thomas R. O'Brien

Our Sunday Visitor Publishing Division
Our Sunday Visitor, Inc.
Huntington, Indiana 46750

Our Sunday Visitor Publishing Division
Our Sunday Visitor, Inc.
200 Noll Plaza
Huntington, IN 46750

ISBN: 1-931709-41-6 (Inventory No. T24)
LCCN: 2002109886

Cover design: Monica Haneline
Interior design: Sherri L. Hoffman
Cover photo: Msgr. Gene Gomulka, author of the Marine Corps and Navy Core Values of "Honor, Courage and Commitment," distributing Communion to Marines.

PRINTED IN THE UNITED STATES OF AMERICA

Table of Contents

Introduction

The initiative for the idea of *Blessings from the Battlefield* was the fruit of a kind of think-tank preparing for the Church's celebration of the new millennium. Pope John Paul II set one weekend aside during the Jubilee to recognize the role played by the military forces of the free world in keeping the peace, and our Archdiocese for the Military Services was to participate.

What might we present to the Holy Father to highlight the distinctive role played by the United States military — and particularly the Catholic presence in our military — in our many and varied attempts to free enslaved people and assure world peace throughout the last century?

Would it not be most fitting to have our present and former Catholic chaplains tell of their most memorable moments as they accompanied our troops and served our military families around the globe? The sacrifices of these priests would well reflect the countless acts of anonymous self-giving on the part of young Americans in uniform dedicated to serve and not be served; to give their lives for the sake of others, even to death; to pursue the vocation of peacemaker.

We were privileged to present a bound copy of these stories to our Holy Father during the Jubilee for the Military, on November 19, 2000.

Many similar, singular pastoral experiences could be related, and many more are being enacted throughout our worldwide archdiocese, even as you read this.

Our Catholic chaplains are drawn from dioceses and religious communities from all over our nation. They volunteer to serve and obtain the permission of their appropriate Church superiors. As noncombatants, their purpose is to provide pastoral care for Catholics in uniform who have a congressionally recognized right to that care. The effort calls for significant sacrifices on the part of our priests, leaving home communities of family, friends, and congregations, encountering rugged, often primitive and dangerous conditions, submitting to the demands of military disciplines and customs. Almost one hundred priests have died in service to our nation during the wars of the twentieth century.

The Catholic chaplain over the years, as will be suggested in the pages that follow, has made the saving difference in millions of young lives by his example of dedication to Christ, His Church, and to the country he loves. The chaplain's call is a vocation within a vocation, with unique opportunities for evangelization on behalf of hundreds of thousands of young military personnel and young families often in search of more meaningful values and guidance. His missionary vocation continues to make a difference in a profession ever in need of reminders of the dignity of every human being, the importance of a moral law even and especially in combat, and the sovereignty of God in every area of life. As Catholics and Americans we can take great pride in our Catholic chaplains and in their collaborating chaplains of other denominations and faith groups.

This book is dedicated to my brother Thomas, to whom belongs its initiative and realization. A former Marine who invested considerable love and talent in the work of our Archdiocese for the Military Services, he died in September of 2001.

May this little work serve as a worthy remembrance of him, as a fitting tribute to our chaplains, and as an encouragement for more priests to step forward in privileged service to God and country.

Archbishop Edwin O'Brien
Washington, D.C.
Memorial Day, 2002

Blessings
from the Battlefield

Photo by Chaplain Gene Gomulka,
author of the Core Values of "Honor, Courage and Commitment"

Martyrs for the Faith

Father Leonard Stegman
(Majonni, Korea)

It was December 1950, and we were some thirty miles west of Wonsan, in a little village called Majonni. Our unit, the First Battalion, Fifteenth Infantry Regiment, had been assigned the task of harassing the enemy and protecting the Korean Marine Battalion west of our position.

Casualties in our unit were devastating, and sub-zero cold and knee-high snow made medical evacuation nearly impossible. Having been denied permission to fight our way out, we knew that any day would bring hordes of Chinese and North Korean Communists who could easily overrun our position. The good people of Majonni were keenly aware of this reality and lived in daily fear.

One day as I walked through the village with a priestly stole in my hand, a civilian approached me, kissed the stole, and led me to the chief of the village. Through an interpreter I learned that the entire village was Catholic, yet hadn't seen a priest for two years. I offered to hear confessions and celebrate Mass for them.

They assembled at two in the afternoon and the entire village lined up to have confessions heard . . . the content of which was known only to the penitent and the Lord, since I didn't understand Korean. I proceeded to offer Mass atop a stack of ammunition crates, and all proceeded well until I announced Holy Communion. The entire congregation objected with vigorous shakes of the head — it was afternoon and they hadn't fasted — until I assured them that I could give them permission to do so.

It was December 4, 1950. The Mass was a very simple and touching ceremony, made more so by the impending danger from the north.

On December 5 we received permission to fight our way out.

On December 6 the North Korean Communists overran Majonni and killed everyone in the village.

Were they martyrs for the faith? I don't know for sure — but I feel confident enough to pray not only *for* the villagers of Majonni but also *to* them. ✠

A Desert Storm
on Christmas

Father David M. Fitz-Patrick
(Dhahran, Saudi Arabia)

Short of an actual firefight, the 1991 Christmas Eve tableau in Saudi Arabia couldn't have been much more bleak. Erratic phone service made it virtually impossible to talk with the folks back home. New terrorist threats were being posted almost hourly.

The last plane bringing holiday mail had come and gone. Our chapel was an underground parking garage.

"Operation Desert Storm" indeed. Rain, which had fallen steadily all day Christmas Eve, had turned into a torrential downpour an hour before midnight. Water began to drip through the ceilings and flow through the holes in the wall. Streams literally ran under our feet in open drainage ditches.

As the only Catholic chaplain in Dhahran, I was beginning to wonder if my British, French, and American "parishioners" in the area would venture out in this kind of weather. But by 11:30 p.m. every seat was filled by the desert-camouflaged congregation, and just before midnight it was "standing room only": almost five hundred fifty people packed into a space designed for thirty cars, with more outside in the rain, eagerly awaiting the start of Mass to celebrate the birth of the Prince of Peace.

A young airman plucked out the notes of Silent Night on a beat-up old guitar as the procession moved toward the altar. It was led by the four-year-old daughter of a local Catholic official. She carried a statue of the Christ child, which she gently placed in a primitive nativity scene in front of the altar.

Looking around I noticed that every face was wet. At first I thought it was from the dripping rain; but as I caught myself getting choked up, I realized that tears were running down everyone's faces. Like me, they were thinking about their families back home, where Christmas was being celebrated in a more traditional setting with evergreens and poinsettias decorating the altar, and church bells ringing out the news of Our Lord's birthday.

As I looked into the faces of the young soldiers, I realized how happy I was to be there as a member of the chaplain service . . . gladly serving as a spiritual caregiver, a visible reminder of the holy, in support of our military family. ✠

Fatherhood

Father Thomas P. Hall
(Sigonella, Italy)

One night the command chaplain had dinner for a couple of other padres and me. The other two guys were visiting Sicily for a few days. I left his place at about 10:30 that evening. I wanted to take the scenic drive up Mount Etna on the way home but discovered a festival blocking traffic and was forced to take the Autostrada. I was ticked.

After less than two miles on the Autostrada, the traffic slowed to a crawl. As I inched forward, I noticed a fire truck and a hearse. I reached into the glove compartment for my oils and began rehearsing in my head how to do the Sacrament of the Sick in Italian. When I finally arrived at the site, the area was filled with Navy security in camouflage uniforms. The carabinieri — the Italian national police — tried to move me on; but when

I explained who I was, they instantly cleared traffic for me.

The victim was a nineteen-year-old sailor from Nebraska. He was thrown from his jeep. No seat belt. The impact, centered on his head, produced one of the most gruesome accidents I'd ever seen. The injuries were so severe that the head fell from the corpse. When I anointed the hands, they were still warm. As I touched his back during the prayer of final committal, I thought of his mother and father back in Nebraska who would soon have their lives shredded by grief.

When the Italian authorities went to remove the body, the other sailors there — mostly in their late teens and early twenties — formed a human wall to block the site from gawking motorists driving by. A noble and spontaneous effort to preserve a bit of personal dignity.

I returned to the base and did what was called a "Critical Incident Stress Debriefing" with the witnesses. It is the first stage of integrating an experience like this into one's memory bank without being paralyzed by the process. I got to bed at two in the morning.

Later in the morning, during my indoctrination talk to newly arrived sailors on the island, I looked out at their young faces and had an epiphany. It was no mistake that I ended up on the Autostrada last night. That poor sailor's dad would have wanted to be with him in this most critical instant of his life. But he wasn't. I was the *Father* there in his stead. To anoint his body, to touch his back, and to pray, "May the angels lead you into paradise. . . ." ✠

'Dear Archbishop...'

Archbishop Joseph T. Ryan
(1913-2000, R.I.P.)
(Beirut, Lebanon)

In 1982, at Christmastime, I visited our Army men and women in the Sinai Desert, our Navy and Marines on the airfield in Beirut, our Air Force in Turkey, and our Navy on five ships in the Mediterranean. Not one of these areas was far from Bethlehem.

On Christmas morning I offered Mass on the airfield in Beirut, where fighting continued to rage. In the bunker where I offered Mass — just eighty miles from the birthplace of the Prince of Peace — I wondered what I could say to these brave young men about Christmas.

After the Mass a young Marine sergeant gave me a Christmas card. I opened it and read these words: "Dear Archbishop, the rams of the Lord's flock are pleased that you came to be with them at Christmas, and thank you for offering Mass for them." I was moved by the message and promised the young sergeant that I'd visit his wife and three small children.

From the airfield in Beirut I went to offer Mass on the warship New Jersey. In preparing the altar and before putting on my vestments, I took out the sergeant's Christmas card again and for the first time glanced at the front of it. The front depicted, in the lower left-hand corner, four Marines carrying a Christmas tree up a slight rise very much like that on Iwo Jima. At the upper right-hand corner was the Star of Bethlehem with its rays forming a cross. In the center of the card were the words "Helping Make It Right," referring, of course, to the Navy and Marines on the airfield in Beirut.

Thinking back to that bunker in Beirut, I need not have worried what to say to those young warriors about their role at Christmas. The front of their Christmas card proved that they knew precisely what they were doing . . . and what American service personnel have been doing during all our wars . . . "Helping Make It Right." ☧

Phone Service

Father Stephen Wagman
(1921-2002, R.I.P.)
(Somewhere in the jungles of Vietnam)

The war in Vietnam was in its early stages. The word had just come down that a soldier on an American artillery base had been killed the night before by incoming mortar fire. I was needed to conduct the memorial service for the deceased.

The rules were very clear: A chaplain was to conduct a memorial service for the deceased as soon as possible after death. Our chopper took off immediately for the dense jungle. After nearly a half-hour in the air, the pilot was able to hover just under treetop level before he silently jerked his thumb toward the open door — the universal sign for "Jump!" — and bellowed over the din of the propellers, "I'll be back to pick you up in thirty minutes!" This was an active Viet Cong stronghold, and the pilot wasn't about to make his favorite tin bird a sitting duck for enemy mortars. By the time I collected myself from the fifteen-foot tumble out the gunner's door, I looked up just in time to see the helicopter fading from sight.

When I looked up a second time, a young captain of the firing artillery battery was standing over me in obvious distress. "Padre, the troops in my battery are scattered over three square miles. It's too dangerous to attempt bringing them all together. We could all be mortared again at any minute. Could you conduct the memorial service by land lines?" he asked. Just as the words spilled from his mouth, a mortar round crashed to the ground not two hundred yards away.

It was clearly time to improvise.

So with telephone handset in one hand, and prayer book in the other, I read the prayers for the dead over the telephone hookup while the crews stood around a squawk box at each artillery piece.

I fervently hoped that each young man could hear my prayers. I'm certain Our Lord did. ✛

We Know That Our
Priest Loves Us

⌒━◆━⌒

Father Michael Zuffoletto
(*Guantánamo Bay, Cuba*)

From October through December 1994 I was assigned to Operation Sea Eagle at the U.S. Naval Station, Guantánamo Bay, Cuba. Our purpose was to provide help and assistance to the thousands of Haitians and Cubans who took to the sea in makeshift boats and rafts seeking greater freedom in the United States. The U.S. Coast Guard was intercepting these primitive craft and bringing the passengers to Guantánamo. Because the majority of those interned were Catholics, the American military assigned numerous priests to travel to Cuba and look after the refugees' spiritual needs.

I was assigned to Camp Romeo, populated by ten thousand Cuban men, women, and children — most of them families. The camp itself was set up in a dry riverbed that was muddy and oppressively hot. Each tent accommodated eight families with virtually no privacy. Something less than the Ritz Carlton Hotel, to be sure.

I attempted to improve the conditions of these people as best I could, given our limited resources. I celebrated Mass each day in Spanish, and recorded it for broadcast over local radio for those camps without a priest. We even managed to form a choir of men, women, and children that sang at Mass and other occasions around the base. For many, it was their first opportunity to participate at Mass in decades. They radiated joy at the ability to receive the Eucharist.

Most days were filled with small humanitarian errands that we hoped might improve morale: trips to the commissary to buy supplies, reuniting family members separated in two different camps, pleading with government officials to allow some refugee to phone relatives already in the United States.

One day a TV crew from Miami arrived to film an "exposé," detailing the tension between the Cuban migrants and the American military. They made it very clear that they would only interview refugees who would speak ill of their treatment at Guantánamo. After screening dozens of Cubans who refused to criticize their lot, the producer became visibly frustrated. When asked why, one of the Cuban men spoke for the rest of the camp, saying: "We have no problems here. We know our priest loves us, and we love our priest."

No matter how long I'm privileged to minister as a priest, that answer will always be in my mind as a tribute to all military chaplains and the work they do. ✢

Death and Dishonor

❦

Father Anthony Trapani
(Somewhere in the Gulf)

I was returning from evening chow, and the mood in every corner of the headquarters compound was somber. We'd just been briefed that Operation Desert Storm would begin at daybreak. Thoughts about what to prepare and how to prepare began streaming through my head. I had no idea what to expect, yet needed to be prepared for it. Whatever "it" was.

At that moment a female soldier walked into the area and asked if she could talk with me. She first let me know that she was representing all the women on the base. They'd been discussing the possible outcomes of the battle that was about to unfold. "We've been talking about what might happen if we're taken prisoners by the Iraqi soldiers . . . and what we'd do if they raped and sexually abused us. I guess we wanted to know what God would think if we killed ourselves rather than be subjected to their rape and sexual abuse."

I think they knew what the padre would say, but they needed to hear it. Their normal human fears were distracting them from the Christ's larger truths. "We know it would be wrong to commit suicide, but under the circumstances we wonder if it would be better than the consequence of being raped," the soldier said.

"Oh, dear God," I thought, "this is it." We began to talk about the ultimate wrongs of suicide and the importance of life. We reflected on the fact that in war (and in captivity) men raped and sexually abused to the same degree as these women feared. We discussed the question of faith in God, trust in self, witnessing to the importance of life, and the willingness to suffer and die for what we believed. These were the words that flowed between us. It was time to be a soldier, to exercise the Code of Conduct, but most of all to trust in the God who would always be present with her, with her friends, and with her fellow soldiers and Marines.

"We knew that was the answer, Father. We just needed to hear you say it." And she left. ✢

'Operator 14'

Monsignor Robert Spiegel
(*Augsburg, Germany*)

It was late on one especially dreary night in Augsburg, Germany, when my phone rang.

"This is Operator 14, Father." The female operator had a very distinctive accent; not German, not American — more what you'd hear in Australia or New Zealand.

"Hello, Operator 14," I replied. "What can I do for you?"

"It's not for me," she said. "It's for a friend of mine. She and her American veteran husband have been married for years. Now he's dying of cancer. He needs to see a priest but cannot seem to find one. Will you visit him?"

"Sure," I said, and asked for the man's name, address, and phone number.

I called him, identified myself as a priest, and asked if I might see him, adding: "A friend of yours gave me your phone number."

"Was it Operator 14?"

"Yes," I replied.

"Then you may visit me if you wish."

When I arrived at his apartment, his wife answered the door. A lady of few words, she introduced herself and pointed to her husband sitting by the window, smoking a cigarette. He coughed and said, "Sit down." I did.

I'd never been in a home with so many beautiful antiques. There was a collector's item everywhere I looked or sat. We talked about the magnificent antiques. "They are that," he said. "Magnificent. We spent a lot of time — too much time — and money collecting them."

As our conversation was coming to an end, I began to mention words that might lead us away from his financial life and allow us to delve into his spiritual life: thornbushes, rocky soil versus good soil, footpaths, seed, Word of God, wind.

"Would you like to get out of the thornbushes, off the footpaths, and out of the rocky soil?" I asked him.

He understood the metaphor right away.

"Yes," he replied, " but I can't. You better go now."

"Can I come back?"

"Yes," his wife replied. To which he added, "Yeah, my wife wants you to. But not more than once a week, okay?" I agreed and left.

In the last days of his life the medication he was taking caused him to stay awake all night and sleep during the daylight hours. When his wife confided that she could hardly take it anymore, I suggested that she hospitalize him for a few days so that she could get some rest.

About a week later, in the middle of the night, my phone rang. "Please come, he's acting up." I arrived to find him standing on the balcony, pitching priceless antiques into the air, down onto the sidewalk, saying, "This is no damn good." He saw me walk into the room, and froze in mid-pitch.

"Okay, I think I'm starting to get my values sorted out. It's time for me to get out of the thorn-bushes and rocky soil . . . and off the footpaths, too."

Then he climbed into bed and received the Sacrament of Reconciliation. He never left the bed again.

His wife was gracious when she phoned me the next day to say that he'd just passed away.

And I'm certain I detected an Australian accent. ☩

A Cancer of Body and Soul

Father Robert Schindler
(Tampa, Florida)

It was fall of 1997 when Mike was admitted to our VA hospital in Tampa with a three-inch tumor just above his left eye. But that was just one of Mike's wounds. He was broke, unemployed, homeless, estranged from his family, and embittered with life in general. Mike was asphyxiating in despair. Despite his refusal of any spiritual ministration, I continued to visit him daily.

His condition took an even more dramatic turn when the medical team announced that the planned surgery on his tumor was fraught with great risk and little potential reward; little could be done to save his sight — or his life. Prepared for Mike's emotional wrath on my next visit to his room, I learned that he'd left the hospital the night before. Not checked out, just walked out.

When Mike returned four days later, I was somehow able to score a spiritual breakthrough.

With deep satisfaction I gave him the sacraments of Penance, Anointing of the Sick, and Holy Eucharist. Now strengthened spiritually and emotionally, Mike decided to proceed with the perilous surgery.

Just prior to the operation Mike asked me to locate his wife somewhere in Florida and get her a little help. With the assistance of the hospital social worker and the Meals-on-Wheels program, we discovered her living in an abandoned pickup truck. Mike was delighted that we were able to get his wife some modest financial assistance, an apartment, and regular nourishment.

After the surgery, Mike received Communion daily. And because he was now completely blind, we were able to get him the Bible on audiotapes. Most important, we were able to locate the couple's only daughter, from whom they'd been estranged for many years. On a visit to Mike's room one day, I found him talking on the phone with his daughter, his face bathed in tears.

The family was now completely reconciled with Christ. And each other.

Before his daughter was able to travel from Colorado, Mike died. However, she did arrive in time to help her mother with the funeral, and return her safely to her new life in Florida. ✠

Straining the Heart Through a Chain-Link Fence

❦

Father Randall Roberts
(Riyadh, Saudi Arabia)

During Operation Desert Storm I was assigned to Escon Village, Saudi Arabia, but had the opportunity to visit many smaller, even more remote sites away from our main base in Riyadh. To my surprise, I discovered a huge number of Filipinos, Hispanics, and Indians working throughout the country. To the American and Saudi governments they were TCNs (Third Country Nationals). To me, they were simply Catholics far from home.

Wishing not to offend our host nation, our government had made it crystal clear that American chaplains would conduct services only for American and allied troops, even then keeping a very low profile. This meant not using clearly recognizable Christian symbols to advertise our worship services — word of mouth only, please —

and removing the religious insignia from our uniforms. But it also meant thousands of Roman Catholic TCNs deprived of the sacraments.

Picture the circumstances under which Mass was normally celebrated: Encircled by a chainlink fence in an abandoned recreation shack with three walls — the fourth long since eliminated by concussion — a Mass kit sits atop a pool table, and officiating is a young priest in camouflage battle dress with only a stole around his neck. Hardly a prestigious setting for the Eucharist. Yet the Mass was always well-attended, generally by troops who had passed the word through the desert that the padre had scheduled Eucharist.

Then one day a TCN happened by. I think he was Filipino, and I don't even know how he had found us. Because the shack was set back from the road, it must have been a stray glance and idle curiosity that drew him closer. But it was his deep faith that glued him to that fence. As I celebrated Mass, my eyes could not help but wander out to that fence, where the young man was pressing himself against it. He appeared to be straining his whole body — or at least his heart — through the chain-link fence, like water through a filter, to make himself more present at a holy ritual he sorely missed and cherished.

The sheer ecstasy on his face from being present at the Holy Sacrifice of the Mass — though not able to move closer — is an image that will be indelibly etched on my heart until I die. That image was a glowing testimony to the ability of great faith to sustain man under the most inhospitable circumstances. ☩

Cathedrals in the Wilderness

❦

Archbishop Edwin O'Brien
(Bien Hoa, Vietnam)

Grace comes in many unexpected ways . . . and at many unexpected moments.

A priest of nine years, theologically well-educated and rather conscientious in my prayer life, I discovered that the jungles of Vietnam provided the occasion for a profound renewal in my love for the Lord's Real Presence in the Eucharist.

My daily routine for seven days a week, two months at a stretch, involved boarding a helicopter from a firebase carved into the jungled mountains, in order to "drop in" on contingents of as many as a hundred soldiers. Each day my Southern Baptist counterpart and I sought to bring the presence of God to a brave cadre of lonely, grungy, but grateful young soldiers whose task was to intercept companies of Viet Cong guerrillas bent on overrunning local villages.

Our companies were on the move every day, necessitating the daily clearing of new landing pads just large enough to receive our chopper, which, by the way, also brought hot meals and mail from home. How many nineteen-year-olds found a new sense of God during their terrifying weeks and months in that wilderness? Virtually all the young troops carried Bibles. Protestants as well as Catholics were eager for the plastic rosary beads I'd bring, and many would hang them from their neck in a tangle with their dog tags. But they were anxious, as well, to speak of fears, of problems — real and imagined — at home, and so often their desire to draw closer to Christ.

It is at that very moment that the Vietnamese jungle becomes a cathedral, with a makeshift altar from a Mass kit set on cardboard boxes. Lectors would rehearse their lines as I would hear a few confessions. Security demanded that all be carried out in very hushed tones. But make no mistake; in that twenty-minute celebration of hungering hearts being sated with the Body and Blood of the Lord, these new young disciples were no less refreshed than when the Lord Himself broke bread for His earliest disciples.

Though these were experiences as unique and indelible as any could be for this priest, a singular grace was my reward when, after two months of this challenging routine, I found myself on a fully developed Air Force base in Bien Hoa. Though I'd been celebrating Mass daily, and often several times daily, I approached the Catholic chapel on base with the dawning realization that during those two months in the bush, I'd never had the opportunity, silently and meditatively, to be still before that Tabernacled Presence so treasured in our Catholic spirituality. Before or since, never have I experienced a richer, more fruitful Holy Hour as I did that morning. And as I reveled in its consolation, I wondered how so many good folks could find their way through life without this Presence.

And I prayed for those who then filled the tropical forests with Communist zeal bent upon demolishing this gift, which alone is able to make us free. ✢

'I Love You, Dad ... But I Want to Go to Heaven'

Father Daniel Leeuw

(Fort Wayne, Indiana)

God has been very generous. He has filled my life with a wealth of human and spiritual adventures. I've been a butcher, a banker, and worked for George Hallas, the Chicago Bears' owner and coach. I've been a high school principal, a college teacher, a parish priest, and a hospital chaplain. But most important I've been an instrument of the Holy Spirit.

Allow me to share just one of many examples of how the Holy Spirit used me in my life as a Catholic chaplain of the military veterans.

On Friday, March 20, 1992, I was visiting the two medical floors of the VA hospital in Fort Wayne, Indiana. With a list of patients in my hands, together with sacramental ritual and oil, I was visiting the Catholic residents of the facility. I passed a room, caught sight of a very young man lying in bed, and sensed the Spirit's movement as He directed me to "visit that man." I checked my list and found that his name wasn't on it, so I continued on my way to visit other patients. After completing my work on the fourth floor, I passed Room 443 again, where that young man appeared to be very ill. Again the Spirit spoke to me, "Visit that man." Touched and moved by the Spirit, I went into that room and introduced myself as the Catholic chaplain. He was cordial, telling me his name, Richard Scott Titus (Scott to his friends), and some facts about his life. He was a career soldier in the U.S. Army who had been stationed in Germany for six years as a food-service specialist. He was just twenty-eight, married with two children: Kathleen, age five, and Anthony, age three.

He became ill in Germany and was diagnosed with cancer of the pancreas. He was sent back to the States and placed in the VA medical center in Fort Wayne near the home of his parents. He'd stopped his chemotherapy treatments, knowing that he was terminal and wanting as much quality time as possible with his family before his death. I gave him my blessing, with a promise to return and help him cross the bridge to eternity.

For the next month and a half I visited Scott twice weekly. We talked together and prayed together, and became friends to the point where he looked forward to my visits.

On one of my last visits with Scott I realized that his life on earth was coming to an end. He had grown so very weak, his body was jaundiced, and his breathing was labored. His wife, parents, and members of the family were keeping vigil. I asked him if he had ever been formally baptized. He responded, "No." He said his parents were Baptists and they left it up to their children to make the decision as an adult. His parents had called their Baptist minister to come and baptize Scott, but the minister found his state in such a weakened condition that he could not be lowered into a pool of water for baptism. So the minister had spoken only the words.

I explained to Scott that one must say the words and pour the water simultaneously in baptism. He responded that he accepted Jesus as his personal Savior, wanted to go to Heaven, and wanted to be baptized. His father objected to my baptizing him. Scott replied by saying: "Dad, I love you, but I do want to be baptized and go to Heaven."

With Scott's request and permission, I asked him the four essential questions about believing in God, in His Son, Jesus, as his Lord and Savior, belief in an eternal life in Heaven, that Christ died for his sins, and that God rewards the good and punishes the evil. Strongly and firmly he asserted his belief, and I baptized him "Richard Scott Titus." He was so happy, bringing tears to my eyes and "Deo Gratias" to my lips and heart.

Scott's father, disturbed, left the room. I joined him in the hall, where he told me he had three children whom he never had baptized, explaining that he had left that commitment up to them upon reaching adulthood. "You have made him a Catholic," he said of Scott, "and this upsets me." I calmed him down, telling him I led Scott to Christ, and now he is a follower of Jesus all the way to Heaven. I added that there is only one baptism, as St. Paul the Apostle has pointed out, and that is baptism into Jesus. He breathed a sigh, saying, "Thank God."

On Saturday evening, April 25, at 8:30, I was at the bedside of Scott, who was dying. I prayed over him and blessed him, and four hours later, on April 26 at 12:30 a.m., he died. When I blessed Scott in his coffin a few nights later, I said, "I'll see you in heaven, Scott." ✞

Charley

Father W. Henry Kenney, S.J.
(*Lexington, Kentucky*)

I've never seen anybody fight for his life the way that Charley did — that's what I'll call him.

Charley had gone through everything possible to conquer cancer. For several weeks, it was apparent that cancer was the clear victor — but Charley held on and on, week after week.

Charley had his larynx removed. He was skin and bones, and he could barely hold himself upright, or even hold onto a pencil. But he could communicate. And what he communicated most clearly tore at my heart: He did not think he could be forgiven.

I served at our VA hospital on Fridays. After each visit with Charley I was convinced it was his last Friday. Never before had I seen the extent to which sheer willpower could perpetuate life.

On what proved to be the final Friday, he was failing noticeably, refusing to do what he did best

— communicate. Now I was moved to give Charley as persuasive a view of Christ's mercy as I knew how; I really laid it on. Afterward, I was very much rewarded to notice Charley communicating again — this time communicating relief.

I, too, was relieved when I saw in the paper that he'd died a day and a half later. I'm not certain that I helped him make the necessary transition, but I was happy for him that he made it.

And happy for myself that I'd had the privilege of knowing such a great man. ☩

'Suffer the Little Children'

Father Vince Inghilterra
(Mogadishu, Somalia)

It was less than three weeks after my arrival in Mogadishu that I came upon a food station and a saint of an Irish nurse named Geraldine. I discovered both in the devastated port area of the city where thousands of children teem through the shattered streets.

Geraldine has a mission in life to make certain that more than a thousand children are fed each day. More than a third of these kids are in the "therapeutic" program, targeted for kids who have less than seventy percent of the body fat and muscle tissue required for their height. All these little creatures subsist on a formula called "Unimix," which is mixed with milk or water in a kettle heated over a twig fire. True, milk is the preferred dilutant; but when milk isn't available — and most times it isn't — water is brought on the back of a mule. The life-giving porridge is administered by Geraldine in plastic bowls twice a day. The tots lap it from their bowls; plastic spoons don't exist here.

If the chemical porridge sounds unappetizing, consider the alternative. The sad reality is that real food would kill them. That tiny digestive metabolism is simply too frail to process nourishment more complex. No matter the medical expertise, one tends to see past their frail bodies and open sores. What is clear to the heart are their broad, welcoming smiles. Amidst all the human degradation, they simply will not allow you to forget that they are children. Smile back and you'll be overwhelmed by hundreds of reaching little hands. Hands that reach for neither money nor food; they simply want to be held. The spectacle breaks my heart.

Geraldine tells me that since the Americans arrived she's been able to get the lifesaving Unimix with some regularity. Before that, shipments were being held captive by local thugs selling it on the black market. The situation became so desperate that one of her staff went down to the port to negotiate with the bandits; he received a bullet in his shoulder for his efforts. With the Americans came hope; at least the children were no longer starving.

While engrossed in play with the children, Geraldine unexpectedly places a one-year-old within my arms. The baby's eyes are swollen shut by starvation. Then Geraldine confirms my worst fears. The child is blind. Oh, God! What kind of world allows this to happen? That night, beneath a silent and starry sky, I thought about that child — starving and blind — and one tear rolled down my cheek, leaving an indescribable and cleansing peace. At least there was one tear shed that night for one child in one unconcerned world. If there was nothing else I could do, at least that was done.

Geraldine is happy that we are here and so are the children. Now I'm happy to be here because it is making a difference. At least now some of the suffering children will survive — a difference on the Somalian front. ✚

Amen in Aden

Father Thomas P. Hall
(Aden, Yemen)

It all started when a young sailor standing watch aboard the USNS Saturn cruising in the Persian Gulf spotted what appeared to be a slick on the surface of the water. Within minutes it was discovered to be a badly decomposed body. By day's end, a total of thirty-two corpses and additional partial remains were recovered from the warm sea.

In Yemen I'd learned from the U.N. High Commissioner for Refugees that a Somali refugee ship had capsized a week earlier, with one hundred eighty passengers reported missing. I'd flown to the Saturn by helicopter, along with two Yemeni imams we'd picked up in Aden, with instructions that every attempt be made to provide burial rites appropriate for the Somali victims, most of whom would be Muslim.

Landing on the deck of the Saturn, we were immediately assaulted by the odor of decay. How humbling to realize that our bodies reduce to the same chemical compounds as common garbage.

The remains of the victims had been placed in plastic bags, then inserted into cardboard boxes. The bodies couldn't be cast into the sea in those wrappings. The cardboard would disintegrate, leaving the bloated bodies to float to the surface in their plastic bags. Additionally, religious exigencies had to be taken into consideration. The imams directed that the bodies be unpacked and identified by gender. The twenty-six women and children were laid out in weighted body bags for burial separately from the men.

While imams sang the prayers of Islam, committing the souls of the deceased to Paradise, I donned a stole and intoned my own Catholic prayer of final committal. Then, one by one, each of the bodies was lowered over the side of the ship and placed gently into the sea facing toward Mecca. The entire process transpired over a period of four hours. It was conducted with the utmost reverence.

I accompanied the imams back to Aden, where they were greeted again by the U.N. Delegation for the High Commissioner for Refugees.

Our farewells were warm. We had been brought together from our respective cultures and religions by a sentiment that was common to us all. "In the end," St Paul writes, "just three things will remain: faith, hope, and love. But the greatest of these is love."

Amen. ✢

The Mistresses of Tublee

Father Thomas P. Hall
(Tublee, Bahrain)

While serving with the U.S. Fifth Fleet in Bahrain, I befriended the local pastor, Father Felicio, a tall, dark-skinned Goan whose winning smile could have launched a career in the cinema.

One night I accompanied him on a parochial visit to some parishioners who, mysteriously, weren't comfortable attending Mass in the big church in central Manama. They live in Tublee, near where the sewage from the capital city spills into the Persian Gulf.

The building we entered was poorly maintained, but the large apartment was tidy, though spare. It consisted of a central hall with four bedrooms opening onto it. There were sixty people waiting for us in a space that might comfortably accommodate thirty. I later learned that twenty people actually live there, mostly Filipino women and children. For an hour Father Felicio and I heard confessions in two adjoining bedrooms, while the din of praying voices ground away at our hearts from the central hallway: "O Mary conceived without original sin, pray for us. . . ."

The Mass was celebrated on All Souls' Day, and one of the older women recited the names of all the deceased for whom the Mass was to be offered. It was an exhausting recitation of Spanish and Filipino names that took nearly fifteen minutes. Not a single name was to be overlooked or forgotten.

When it came time for Communion, only a handful of those present partook. It was later explained by Father Felicio that most of these women were "mistresses" of one or more Bahraini men. They had fled the Philippines because of the exigencies of survival. In the Persian Gulf countries money is plentiful, and for those with no skills to barter, there is always the body.

When we left the building well after midnight, we were given bouquets of flowers. Huge commercial — not backyard — bouquets for which we pay seventy-five dollars or more back in the States. And food. They piled enough lumpia and pancet (popular Filipino dishes) into the van to feed fifty hungry people. Their most touching gesture was to take our hands into their own, pressing them to their foreheads and lips.

I will always remember the mistresses of Tublee, that group of working women who'd come together to worship God and pay homage to the souls of their "faithful departed." I will remember the flowers, the food, and the kisses to my hands. I will remember what they did to feed their children.

And I will never forget that they felt unworthy to receive the Body of Christ . . . unworthy to even enter the big church downtown. ✢

'Thanks, Father, for Making It Possible for Me to See Jesus'

Father John Minkler
(Albany, New York)

One Saturday afternoon in the spring I received a call that a patient in the infectious disease ward of the local VA hospital wanted to speak with a priest.

Observing the required VA hospital protocol for that ward, I donned mask, gown, and rubber gloves before entering the patient's room. There I discovered a young serviceman dying of AIDS. He was barely twenty-five.

Until this point he had rejected any chaplain contact. As I sat by his bed, he told me a sad but familiar story. He had been totally rejected by his family — especially his father — who simply could not deal with the implications of the horrible disease he'd contracted. Finally he broke into tears and asked that I call his family and plead with them to come to him. Then he indicated that he wanted to receive the sacraments of Reconciliation and Communion.

Seeing his grave condition, after administering the sacraments, I rushed to a phone in the hallway to call his family.

When I returned to his room, he said to me, "Thank you, Father, for making it possible for me to see Jesus."

He died just six hours later, with his mother at his side. ✠

'I Pray Daily for Everyone I Killed in Combat'

Monsignor John FitzGerald
(Camp Pendleton, California)

As a chaplain with a Marine Corps infantry battalion, a priest meets many wonderful people. One particular Marine stands out in my memory. Let's just call him Bob.

Bob was a highly decorated staff sergeant with many medals for combat heroism: a Silver Star, three Bronze Stars, and four Purple Hearts for wounds in combat. An especially devout man, he attended daily Mass whenever possible.

There were times when the calls and appointments at the office would run too close to the announced time for Mass, and I'd find myself literally running to the chapel to vest and begin Mass. Bob would already be there, kneeling before the Blessed Sacrament. He'd participate in the liturgy with great attention, and even remain afterward for a period of thanksgiving as I was dashing off to my next appointment.

One day I jokingly said to Bob, "Hey, you're starting to make me look bad. I'm the one who rushes in and rushes out. And you're the one praying privately before and after the Mass. I should take a page out of your book." He laughed, then shared that he not only enjoyed the Mass and his prayers but said the Rosary every day while he ran for exercise. When I asked how long he ran, he replied, "As long as it takes me to pray all fifteen decades of the Rosary."

Bob explained that he'd had several tours of duty in Vietnam, with a lot of time "in country" in the jungle. "I've seen some pretty horrible things," he said, "and had to do some pretty horrible things to survive. I pray daily for everyone I had to kill in combat. In fact I pray daily for everyone who died in Vietnam — on both sides."

Bob was a very strong, physically fit man. The type of unusually handsome Marine you'd select for a recruiting poster. In fact, it was Naval surgeons who'd reconstructed his face from pretty ghastly combat wounds so that he had a pleasant countenance and a wonderfully quick smile. Despite a lisp from a wound to his tongue, Bob never used his gift of speech to complain about his injuries or what his country had called on him to do.

I've often reflected that we'd asked too much of Bob, and probably hundreds of thousands of Bobs whom I never had the privilege of knowing. Whenever I think back on Pope Paul VI's cry at the United Nations, "War. War. War. Never again," or his challenge, "If you truly desire peace, then work for justice," I always think of Bob . . . a great Marine, an exemplary Catholic. ✢

Father John

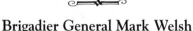

Brigadier General Mark Welsh
(*A story about Father John Pearson in Saudi Arabia, as told to the cadets of the U.S. Air Force Academy by their Commandant of Cadets, Brigadier General Mark Welsh*)

Your first aerial combat sortie is an intensely personal experience.

First of all, it happens at one thousand miles an hour of closure. It's hot fire, cold steel, instant death, big destruction. It's the exhilarating, soaking fear that you'll never see at your kids' ballet recital or soccer game. Ever.

That's why I needed Father John Pearson around my Fourth Fighter Squadron. He was a Catholic priest, and our unit chaplain.

The first day of Operation Desert Storm I walked out in the predawn blackness, and as I reached my jet on the ramp, there was Father John, at the nose of my F-15. Until I got close enough to see who he was, I thought he was the crew chief. But no, it was Father John, bigger than life.

And he was bigger than life. Father John was the first man to buy you a whiskey, the first guy to light up a cigar. He was the first guy to start up a party, and the last guy to leave that party. More important, he would've been the first guy to wade into hell in his BVDs to pull you out if you needed him to. We knew Father John real well, and he fit in great with the fighter squadron.

As I got to the airplane, Father John just said, "Hey, I thought you might like a blessing before you go." Now although I consider myself fairly comfortable in my religion, I immediately began to hate myself. I'd never even thought of that — just too many other priorities on my mind. So I knelt down right there on the cement in front of the jet to receive Father John's blessing.

After I'm done with the preflight of the air-plane and getting ready to climb up the ladder, I notice these other pilots running up out of the darkness to get Father John to bless them, too. So he did.

When we got back from the sortie, we just kind of decided, "That's it. Father John has to bless everybody. Can't change that." And it did-n't matter whether you were Jewish, Baptist, or

Islamic. It just didn't matter: Father John gave the blessing for the Fourth Fighter Squadron whether you flew at two in the afternoon or two in the morning, or any time in between.

I don't know how he did it, but he did it. Every time I landed from a combat sortie, too. Every single time my canopy would open, I'd shake the hand of my crew chief and there, at the bottom of the ladder, would be Father John to bless me and welcome me home.

When I came back home from Desert Storm, I ended up as a single ship returning to Hill Air Force Base. When I pulled into the parking spot and popped my canopy, there was my crew chief on the ladder — and Father John, my wife, family, and friends on the tarmac. I'd written my wife, Betsey, about Father John and his blessings. You want to know how cool my wife is? When I came down the ladder, she turned to him and said, "After you, Father John." Father John walked over, I knelt, and he blessed and welcomed me home.

Eighteen months later Father John dropped dead of a massive heart attack. Fifteen of the twenty-eight pilots who flew in my squadron in Desert Storm were at his funeral in Stockton, California. They came from Korea, they came from Europe, they came from Australia, and they came from all over the United States.

They came to tell his family about Father John. But they also came to bless him and ask God to welcome Father John home. ✢

Return of the Prisoners

Father Robert Fosselman
(*Somewhere in the Philippines*)

The rain had let up as a group of medics, chaplains, Red Cross workers, and well-wishers on the tarmac somewhere in the Philippines watched the heavy, overcast sky. The group was waiting anxiously as the skies parted a little and an olive-green C-147 rescue plane circled carefully and slowly settled on the field. The hatch opened, and the cargo was let down gently on the tarmac.

One by one, stretchers with prisoners-of-war released from a Japanese POW camp in Manchuria were carefully, almost reverently, received by the medics. Most were woefully emaciated, but some were able to struggle down the ladder on their own.

As I recall, from somewhere a few musical instruments had been hastily gathered and a little band broke into "The Star-Spangled Banner."

Prisoners who could, feebly attempted to give a salute, and through the tears the welcoming assembly of GIs and Filipinos gave a great cheer.

What a surprise it was to see among the prisoners Father Alvin LaFeir. Father Alvin had been a sometime assistant pastor at St. Mary's in Huntington, Indiana, when I was a student there. Father Alvin, in a daze, gave no sign of recognition.

The released prisoners were taken to the evacuation center and in a three-day process given nourishment, though they could scarcely eat any of the food until they slowly adjusted to the diet prepared.

Visiting Father Alvin after the medics had processed and cared for him two days, I was thrilled that he finally had regained some of his mental and psychological health. He recognized me, and before he left we were able to resume the friendship of the past. Father Alvin had been taken captive on Guam, a U.S. possession in the Western Pacific, and transported to Manchuria, where, as I recall, he spent four long years as a POW. It was a poignant moment to be there at the release of these American soldiers and civilians. ✠

The Sounds of Healing

Father Jerome Sommer
(Cam Ranh Bay, Vietnam)

It was on February 10th that I landed in that country in ninety-degree heat. In less than twenty-four hours, we lost not only a day in crossing the dateline, but all of winter and spring as well. I was as safe as one can be in Vietnam — probably safer on that desert-like strip of sand than you are when you drive on the highway. The war went on out there somewhere a few miles away, but even the Vietcong seemed to have sense enough not to want to inhabit that place.

After landing at Bien Hoa airport twenty-two miles northeast of Saigon, I spent two days at a replacement battalion — not exactly the Hilton Hotel. It was designed, one could conclude, to brainwash newcomers into thinking that anywhere else in Vietnam must be an improvement.

On Sunday, two days later, the Air Force packed a bunch of hot and dusty soldiers into space meant for cargo but not for people. Jonah must have felt about as comfortable inside that whale. We flew up-country, north of Saigon, where the airborne whale disgorged its contents. A bus towed me and my baggage the final few miles to my destination on the east coast of the country, a narrow and sandy peninsula with the South China Sea on one side and Cam Ranh Bay on the other. If your map of this part of the world is big enough, it marks the spot as Cam Ranh Bay, 12 degrees north latitude and 109 degrees east longitude. Though not well-suited for living purposes, it is strategic militarily, for the bay is one of the best harbors in the world, and we had begun to exploit its possibilities with the construction of many docks. We appeared to be preparing for a long, long stay.

The Sixth Medical Center was a convalescent hospital capable of caring for one thousand patients. At that time there were eight hundred patients, most recovering from malaria but some from other diseases and battle wounds. The hope was to restore them to health and return them to their units elsewhere.

I had taken the place of a priest who departed for the States soon after my arrival. A Protestant chaplain was there, too, and we got along fine. Our chapel was a hospital ward with homemade benches instead of beds. For Lenten penance, we knelt not on cushioned kneelers but on the concrete floor. The Protestant chaplain played a lot of Bach fugues and such — I'm a Beethoven man myself — and the GIs in the next ward played whatever they call that noise. The combination, in high decibels, was a weird cacophony. Add the racket of Army trucks, helicopters, and low-flying jets from the nearby airbase, and the whole concoction was enough to make Arturo Toscanini turn somersaults in his tomb.

There was one sound missing: the sound of mortars bursting in our midst. For that I was grateful. ✠

An Easter Resurrection

Monsignor William Dendinger
(Tokyo, Japan)

On Easter Monday of 1972 in Japan I went to the office early hoping to do a few things quickly before taking the rest of the day off. After Holy Week services I wanted a few hours to relax and reflect on all the Holy Week activities around the base. As I was about to leave the office, an airman rushed in and said, "Father, there's two hundred dollars missing from the collection." My facial expression quickly communicated that I really wasn't looking forward to spending Easter Monday with the money counters.

As the airman left, the phone rang. "This is Sergeant Conley of the Air Force Audit Agency. I'll need to see you immediately. It's urgent." Assuming he was also concerned about the collection, I agreed to see him within the hour. That two-hundred-dollar shortfall seemed to set off alarms all over the islands of Japan.

When Sergeant Conley arrived, there were tears in his eyes. He clearly wasn't there to talk about money, and began to pour out his heart. The day before, on Easter Sunday, he and his wife had a serious and heated argument. The quarrel had begun at dinner when his wife burst out, "Who are we? Some kind of pagans? Here it is, Easter Sunday, and our children don't even realize it."

He then began to describe their family life. He was Catholic by background, his wife a marginally affiliated Protestant. Married by a justice of the peace, they'd agreed to get involved with the Church later. Now, after fifteen years and three unbaptized children, religious faith was not part of their family. For some reason, this particular Easter Sunday had triggered some reflection about their spiritual life, or lack of it — perhaps living in Japan among the Japanese people had something to do with it. After the heated exchange, he assured her that he'd talk with the Catholic chaplain the next morning.

Now comes the Easter inspiration. I began a series of discussions with the entire family: father, mother, and each of the three children ranging in age from three to twelve years. Because the family dynamic was healthy, they were highly receptive to discussing religion. The children, who were eager to learn, sensed their folks' excitement about becoming active in the Catholic Church, as well. Since the Rite of Christian Initiation had yet to become part of the Church practice in 1972, we scheduled several family sessions before integrating the children into CCD classes.

Over the next eighteen months it seemed that we were celebrating one of the sacraments for some member of this particular family every Sunday. On one such Sunday the mother was baptized and received First Communion. On the following, the parents had their marriage validated, to the joy and applause of the entire community. Soon after, the three children were baptized. Two weeks later, the two older children received First Communion, and the oldest was confirmed by the bishop, along with her mother.

In 1972 we were accustomed to seeing Catholics being baptized as children and growing up in the Church. Over and over, parishioners commented that they'd never before seen an entire family enter the Church. And the Conleys certainly did enter the Church as an entire family. In addition to their sacramental life, they became very involved with Church life. The mother, who had an excellent musical background, joined the choir and later served as cantor. The father, Sergeant Conley, soon became an usher and got involved in the finances of the parish. The children blended quickly into Church youth activities.

In 1975 the family was transferred back to the United States, where they continued to be involved in the Church, first in the base chapel and later, after Sergeant Conley's retirement, in the civilian Catholic Church in northern California. I managed to stay in touch with them for nearly fifteen years, watching them grow spiritually, emotionally, and chronologically as all three children graduated from college and branched off to nurture strong Catholic families of their own somewhere in the world.

The moral of the story: As the Gospel has taught us over and over, you can always count on wonderful spiritual surprises during the Easter season. In 1972 in Japan, it was an Easter Monday irritant that became a spiritual resurrection for an entire family.

(In case you were wondering, the money was found. It was simply an accounting error.) ✢

The Heavenly Scent of Diesel

Father John Bowe

(Fort Indian Town Gap, Pennsylvania)

Missioned at Fort Indian Town Gap in Pennsylvania for annual summer training in June 1999, I'd decided to make a pastoral visit to the mobile kitchen tent in the woods.

Perhaps to an even greater extent than for regular Army troops, who are better acclimated to the privations of the field, a mobile kitchen tent is often considered morale headquarters for the citizen-patriots of the National Guard. Yet preparation of untold thousands of field meals is frequently one of the Army's least appreciated labors.

It was a few minutes before 5:00 a.m. as I ducked under the flap of the tent hidden deep among the fragrant pines and inhaled the competing aromas of the mobile kitchen tent. Fuel feeding the cookstove, detergent scouring the soup cauldrons, and coffee percolating inside the canvas walls all fused into a singular fragrance that smells like home to hungry field armies the world over.

Relishing the quiet, I sat on a bench at a corner table waiting for the sunrise and the troopers the sun would bring with it. It was then that a soldier, bleached white by the fatigue of a twelve-hour shift preparing breakfast in the tent, approached to request the Sacrament of Reconciliation. He had only a few minutes before his transportation would arrive to take him back to a shower and some rest.

As I was hearing his confession, a mammoth "six-by" troop transport backed up to the tent. As soon as he received his penance, he was immediately rejuvenated. He vaulted over the tailgate of the huge truck, and as I finished making the Sign of the Cross, the truck rumbled down the road, leaving me in a cloud of exhaust fumes.

This time it was a diesel scent commingling with the complex aromas of the mobile kitchen tent that was a — dare I say "Heaven scent"? — reminder of my real purpose in life as a priest-chaplain. ✢

A Mass Jump

Father Charles Gallagher
(Camp Drum, New York)

Eleven paratroopers dead, according to the radio bulletin in the medical aid tent.

The story of this deadly parachute drop over upstate New York was getting out before the Army brass could contain it. Now the medical corpsmen were cleaning up the resulting carnage.

"And now the news.

"Just twenty-eight days into this new year of 1952, tragedy has struck nearby Camp Drum. Eleven paratroopers were killed this morning when their parachutes failed to open at a spectacular cold weather assault exercise here in upstate New York.

"Spectators, who'd gathered to witness six hundred troops of the 188th Airborne Infantry Regiment of Fort Campbell,

Kentucky . . . seeing ten or more unopened parachutes crash to the ground . . .
thousands of feet in the air. . . ."

As chaplain for the 188th Airborne Infantry
Regiment, I was the second trooper through the
door of the huge transport, and saw a calamity in
the making, firsthand. For days, the media had
been eager to witness the coordinated Army and
Air Force jump of an entire battalion. The troops
themselves, however, were less thrilled jumping
from too many planes, in chutes packed by unfa-
miliar hands, onto ground frozen harder than the
sands of Kentucky had ever been.

And consider the interservice rivalry. Air
Force pilots, bristling at the public attention lav-
ished on their Army brethren, threatened to take
off without us if we delayed. (One pilot ultimately
did take off without a single paratrooper on board.)

The rush to take off raised another red flag.
For the first time ever, experienced paratroopers
were not checking their chutes on the ground, but
in the plane at twenty-five thousand feet. It was
much too late to avert disaster at that juncture.

Forty-five minutes into the flight, as the
jumpmaster gestured down to the white ("all
clear") smoke whipping over the drop zone, the

troops pushed three huge bundles of canvas tents through the open doors without chutes. Less than a minute later, I threw my static line, pivoted, and jumped. Looking up to check my canopy I saw that it had opened completely. But bad news arrived on a sudden gust of wind — other troopers were drifting into my chute lines. In the few seconds that it took to steer away from them, I realized that the high winds were causing midair collisions for three miles all around me.

When I finally looked down to see the earth rocketing up toward me, I tried to go limp, then hit hard on my left side. Very hard.

Strong winds were making it impossible for me to collapse my chute after the hit. I could only hold on to the risers as I bumped along the ground, the reserve chute on my chest acting like runners on a sled. I stopped only when another officer grabbed my canopy and collapsed it. Now we both began to race after other troopers as they continued to smash into the frozen ground.

Walking around somewhat dazed, I found a trooper who was cut, bleeding, and quite sense-less. Eventually a litter jeep brought both of us to the aid station. Going from litter to litter I encountered three men with broken legs in a matter of minutes. One correctly diagnosed the impact of his splintered thigh bone on his Airborne career. "I guess this will end my jumping, Chaplain," he said through teeth chattering from cold and pain. Another, on the verge of shock, was repeating, "The bugger didn't open. It just didn't open." Of course, his chute did open or else he wouldn't be sitting there shivering, but his brain couldn't process that information.

Now I began to piece together the facts from the medical reports. Sixty troopers sustained bruises and broken bones. Some serious, all preventable. Eleven fatalities? Actually, none at all. Spectators had mistaken tent bundles for paratroopers as they plunged to earth with unopened parachutes.

Why did the brass approve a jump in wind velocity nearly double the allowable fifteen miles an hour? Budget, press, and spectators were certainly a few of the ingredients in the mix.

How were fatalities avoided under such impossibly hazardous jump conditions? I think you know the answer to that: God is alive and well in upstate New York. ✣

Saving Gonzalez

Father Jeldo J. Schiavone
(Bimba Island, Vietnam)

I volunteered for the chaplaincy because both my brothers were in the Army and I didn't want them to feel I was "ducking" behind the priesthood. The dilemma was that my bishop wouldn't release me until I found a priest to replace me. After several years and a new bishop, I was able to finally meet my commitment and became a military chaplain.

This endeavor took me to Vietnam, where I found myself more like a Christ figure bringing comfort to the men in the battalion. My duties entailed quite a lot of counseling, and I even became a tour guide to Bimba Island near Cam Ranh Bay.

All was going well — even the commander couldn't thank me enough for the incredible treatment I was giving the men. Until one afternoon . . .

Gonzalez, one of the soldiers, had gone totally berserk. He stole an M-16 rifle and ammo, and was starting to shoot at everything around him. The provost marshal summoned both Protestant and Catholic staff duty chaplains, but Gonzalez was Puerto Rican and no one spoke a word of his language. Because I spoke a little Spanish, the provost marshal motioned me to approach the soldier with my arms extended, making it clear I had no weapons. I cautiously communicated to Gonzalez that if he didn't release his weapon the sharpshooters would hit him in both arms. After twenty minutes (it seemed more like twenty hours!), Gonzalez finally fired the remaining rounds into the ground, tossed his M-16 to me, and walked with his hands crossed in surrender.

Three weeks later I received an award for heroism. Personally, I saw it as a willingness to serve my country even at great risk to my life.

The chaplaincy has been a challenge to me. As they told us in chaplain school, "Be ready to be all things to all men." To some at Cam Ranh, I was the padre; to others I was the tour guide. To Gonzalez, I was the mediator. And saving Gonzalez's life was a greater reward than any medal the Army could provide. ✣

The Alphabet of Ministry

Father Thomas Sandi
(Tuzla, Bosnia)

Celebrating the Eucharist and offering the sacraments to hundreds of servicemen is paramount for me as a priest-chaplain. But, as the only Air Force chaplain in this multinational NATO setting in Bosnia, I address the human condition for other faith groups as well. The following "ministry alphabet," outlining just one week's counseling, may illustrate the point that God is very much alive here at Eagle Camp, Tuzla, Bosnia.

Army trooper "A" rediscovers his Protestant faith and becomes a choir soloist.

Air Force civilian "B" attends Monday night Epic videos; afterward shares his conversion story.

Air Force trooper "C" needs to talk in the flight terminal before going home on emergency leave. After receiving my blessing he says, "Chaplain, may I pray over you?"

Marine trooper "D," with a newborn back home, is ashamed because he fears combat.

Turkish trooper "E" introduces himself as a Muslim but insists on affirming the Christians at table. He says, "There is only one God! We must all work for God's peace."

Bosnian civilian "F" tells a table full of American officers how much their presence means to his people, especially the children.

Italian troopers "G" and "H" volunteer to use the firehouse stove to cook a birthday meal for the chaplain in gratitude for being able to participate in the Eucharist.

Tuzla preteen "I" points to himself and sadly whispers, "No father."

Army troopers "J," "K," and "L" are deeply unhappy with their jobs, their relationships, their lives.

Army trooper "M" wonders about his standing out as a Jew in a Christian society.

Air Force trooper "N" ponders how a "pass over" to the next rank will affect his Air Force future.

Navy trooper "O" indicates he is an atheist but is very happy that chaplains are in the camp.

Air Force trooper "P" is uncomfortable as a female in an "all-male environment."

Finnish trooper "Q" is concerned about his young wife, whom he left at home more than a year ago.

German trooper "R" wonders how to motivate troops with a morale problem.

Air Force trooper "S" is painfully lonely because she cannot "fit in" on the job.

Army trooper "T" is uncertain of his decision to make the Army his career.

Air Force trooper "U" is in a troubled relationship and is concerned about reunion.

Russian trooper "V" proudly announces, "We too have chaplains."

Army trooper "W" is trying to come to terms with the suicide of a fellow MP.

Air Force troopers "X" and "Y" ask to become Catholics and seek chaplain confidentiality.

Air Force trooper "Z" wants desperately to talk about his Army buddy who committed suicide in the camp last week. ✣

Tattoo

❦

Father Edward T. Hill
(Zagreb, Bosnia)

In Bosnia, two Canadian soldiers ambushed while driving a truck were rushed to our United Nations hospital tent for triage. I immediately anointed both men. One soldier, who had been shot in the chest, was rushed into surgery. I stayed with the second young man, who had a large-caliber bullet pierce a particularly graphic tattoo on his upper left arm. The doctors were studying his X-rays and considering his options, because they wanted to avoid amputation.

Despite the sudden shock of being shot and the ache in his arm, the young soldier was alert. But he was anxious about his buddy, confused about the events, having difficulty integrating his experience in the med-evac helicopter and the hospital. His eyes were full of tears as he glanced at his heavily bandaged bicep and said to me, "My mother hated that tattoo."

Softly I spoke with him, telling him that a mother's prayers are almost always heard. "Next time tell her not to pray so hard. She almost got you killed," I said. He laughed for the first time, and the pain seemed to disappear, for he saw the truth of this lesson. "I'll tell her that," he responded, then began to weep again.

Miraculously, both soldiers were saved. Grateful for the efficacy of the sacraments and the healing power of prayer, they were transferred home to Canada. But before boarding the plane for Montreal, the soldier with the almost whole arm hollered the length of the passenger ramp, "Father, first thing when I see my Mom, I'm going to tell her about her mother's prayer."

May the comforting words always come so readily. ✠

To Rescue the Rescuers

Father Thomas P. Hall
(Somewhere in the Persian Gulf)

It isn't often that a chaplain can stay up all night glued to his TV until three in the morning. But given the news bulletins that peppered European programming, I could do nothing else. A giant airbus registered to Gulf Air, en route from Cairo, had crashed in Bahrain. Naturally my first thoughts turned to the many friends I have in that tiny emirate — most of whom vacation in Egypt. My next thoughts turned to the U.S. Fifth Fleet that, because of our vast resources in the area, would almost certainly be called into play during the rescue-and-recovery efforts.

The next morning, even before I got my coffee, I got the word: "Grab your seabag and passport. You're on your way to Bahrain." The orders weren't a complete surprise; I was a member, with seven highly trained trauma specialists, of an

"Intervention Response" team. The team's objective: "rescue the rescuers" from the personal trauma they frequently suffer during their disaster recovery efforts. Coping with such gruesome experiences and recouping from them can be as life-shattering for the rescuers as it is for some victims.

I did three debriefs each day, each two hours long, and each more horrific than the last. A young female helicopter pilot, transfixed by the disaster, remained at the crash site for more than eight hours, praying as each body was brought ashore that there be at least one survivor. The last recovery was that of an eight-year-old boy still fully clothed in shorts and Mickey Mouse T-shirt. A burly Marine gunnery sergeant carried the tiny dead body from the shallow water to the ambulance, laid him on the gurney, then tucked in his shirt. "He looked like a doll," the sergeant said.

Words fail when I attempt to express my admiration for our sailors and Marines. The disaster occurred at the start of a long holiday weekend, when these young warriors — like their counterparts the world over — briefly attempt to party their cares away. Our Navy was the first on the disaster scene. As the Bahraini Defense Force stood by, watching in horror, our own sailors and Marines began recovering bodies and body parts.

And they kept at it throughout the night, before the 130-degree desert sun could wreak further havoc on the scene the following morning.

Many of these young American heroes arrive in the military with poor academic records, and even worse family histories. (Some of those stories could fill another chapter, and would curl your hair well before you reach the last page.) But they daily prove themselves capable of the most heroic of acts. At each debriefing, I tell the men the complete and unvarnished truth: I'm privileged to be one of the few Americans to have witnessed their heroism and shaken their hands. ✢

Simple Notes

❦

Father Joseph Duc Vu
(Detroit, Michigan)

"Father, your visits to Rudy and our family during his stay at Veteran's Hospital, and your encouragement meant a lot to all of us. He needed the connection to the Lord that you gave him."

Betty T. and family
March 29, 2000

"Father, you formed a special bond with my dad and daily visited with him during his stay at V.A. As my dad moved into critical stages near the end of his life, you stepped up your efforts to comfort both my dad and my mom. Your efforts were greatly appreciated."

Terrence K.
May 2, 1994

"Father, you left your bed at 3:00 a.m. and made a trip to the bedside of a dying man you did not know. You are a messenger from God."

Bill and Mary Ann V.

July 10, 1997

'Hey, Faddah!'

Father John Kaul
(Camp Lejeune, North Carolina)

On a dark morning in the pouring rain of February, I was driving through the wilds of the Camp Lejeune exercise areas in search of an infantry battalion whose Protestant chaplain had requested Mass for his Catholic troops on this Sunday in the field.

Slogging through the mud in the dark and cold, with the field Mass kit slung over my shoulder under the dripping rain parka, I finally found the tent in which a dozen Marines sat silent on field chairs. All were in the same position — sitting ramrod straight with their M-16s in their right hands, helmets steadied by hand on their left knees. A kerosene heater warmed the chilly dimness lit by a single light bulb above. Someone had done a fine job of creating an altar out of connex boxes, placed a marginally white cloth over the top and arranged a cross and chalice, paten, and missal. With the rain pattering overhead and the readings full of baptism imagery ("fishers of men"), how could I screw this up?

We had a good, prayerful liturgy together and spent some time in conversation afterward. It was warm and comfortable, and no one really wanted to leave. But eventually one of the Gunnies came looking for them, so they began to file out of the tent one at a time. As the last one was about to disappear through the flap, he stopped and turned around to me: "Hey Faddah!" (He was from Brooklyn.) "Hey Faddah!" he said. "Tanks fer findin' us."

This ministry has awesome rewards. ✢

By the Numbers

Father Eric Albertson
(Fort Bragg, North Carolina)

My first assignment as a Catholic chaplain was to Fort Bragg, North Carolina, with the Eighty-Second Airborne Division. This was an exciting unit, and I greatly enjoyed the intensity surrounding this ministry. Yet I was disappointed with the low attendance at my field Masses. I knew that the shortage of priests in the Army was critical but wondered why so few soldiers attended Mass. I later discovered this was normal. Mass is celebrated while the mission is ongoing, so not everyone can attend.

One day while celebrating Mass for paratroopers just off the Salerno Drop Zone, the expected small numbers attended. As was my custom, I offered confession; one soldier, who'd been away from the Church for a number of years, asked to go to confession. I then celebrated Mass and spent a few minutes with him before he went away, obviously content.

Perhaps it was my pride, but I left that field site wondering if I should even remain on active duty. After all, I'd left civilian congregations where I'd often preached to thousands. With the numbers of attendees at my Army Masses, I wasn't sure if my presence was making a difference.

That Sunday, I saw this soldier at Mass with his wife and new baby. She was glowing with excitement at his return to the practice of his faith. We spoke only a moment, but he reminded me that we should soon touch base to schedule the baptism of his daughter.

During the following week, an Air Force F-16 fighter jet crashed into a cargo plane as it prepared to board paratroopers for a jump. Twenty-three men died that afternoon and more than a hundred were seriously burned. Among the dead was the young soldier I'd just ministered to. I was stunned. In the course of a single week, I'd heard his confession, given him final Holy Communion, and anointed him as he lay on the tarmac.

Later his wife and I discussed this soldier's abrupt reversal to faith, and we were simultaneously mystified and grateful. Yet the truth was eventually clear to me. It was not about the numbers of people we reach as chaplains. Rather it's trusting in God to place us where we can touch those He designates most in need of a priest.

So whether we touch a thousand people or just one, I've learned: "Don't count the numbers." ✠

'I'm Hit, Father . . . I'm Dying'

Archbishop Joseph T. Ryan
(1913-2000, R.I.P.)
(Vietnam)

In every priest's life, there are events etched for-
ever in memory.

In mine, as a priest for fifty-three years, it was
the tragic death of an altar boy.

In fact, not any altar boy. He was my altar
boy. And not a boy, either. He was Corporal
George Pace, United States Marine Corps.

The year was 1963. I was a Navy chaplain
serving with the Third Marine Division in Vietnam, and George was my bodyguard. Whether we
liked it or not, wherever I went he went. And we
liked the arrangement, both of us. He'd drive the
jeep to all the areas I covered along the Demili-
tarized Zone between North and South Vietnam.
The troops usually knew when I was coming and
welcomed us warmly.

As a chaplain, I carried no weapons and depended on George for my safety and protection. He carried both an M-15 rifle and a 45-caliber pistol and was responsible for preparing the area and setting up my Mass kit.

It was July 4, a day of relaxation for most Americans, a day of death for George. The place was our home chapel in Dong Ha. I was saying Mass in our little thatched-roof chapel, and gave Holy Communion to George first, then to the other Marines.

A mortar round, fired from North Vietnam just a few hundred yards beyond the DMZ, hit just behind our chapel as we began to serve the Eucharist to other Marines. I was hit in the back with shrapnel, George was hit in the chest. His last words were, "I'm hit, Father . . . I'm dying."

He lay in my arms and died a heroic death. I cannot ever forget him.

"May his soul, and all the souls of brave men who die in the service of their country, rest in peace. Amen." ✝

Grocery Run

Father Lawrence C. Smith, S.J.
(Kuwait City, Kuwait)

The Second Battalion, Fourth Marines, had been in the country for weeks, but our first trip into the city to deliver humanitarian aid was an adventure into the unknown. The primary unknown: snipers. What was the sniper threat, if any? The colonel wasn't certain, but he wasn't about to take any chances, either.

Our first convoy was led by a heavy-guns vehicle. Behind that was my Humvee, with me, my aide, and the sergeant in charge of our scout sniper platoon. Then came a five-ton truck loaded with supplies, another Humvee with seven more scout snipers, and, bringing up the rear, another heavy-guns vehicle. When the sergeant in charge of the snipers was asked by one of his men about the rules of engagement for the city, Sergeant Chase answered quietly, "If somebody shoots at you, kill them." Donning helmets and flak jackets, we moved onto the highway.

The roads were fairly empty except for the military vehicles and children. The kids would run out in front of the fast-moving convoy, forcing it to screech to a stop so they could beg for food. I clearly recall one ten-year-old boy standing in the middle of the highway with his legs spread wide, facing traffic with a Kuwaiti flag raised high over his head. He had no fear of death.

When we got to the church in the city, we found that the British had already arrived. I'll never forget the scene. As we drove into the courtyard next to the church, a British bagpiper was standing on the porch playing away, the crowd around him singing martial music. As we pulled up, they even began singing the Marine Corps hymn. The bishop welcomed us graciously, gave us a tour of the facility, and introduced us to his volunteers.

Thus began a relationship that lasted for months. We ended up bringing a total of ten truckloads of food and supplies that essentially kept the people fed and reasonably healthy until the city came to life again. It was on our last trip to the city that an old lady, holding her rosary beads, met us in the courtyard. She had tears in her eyes. She took my hands in hers, and looking up, said, "Thank you."

That made it all worthwhile. ✢

A Calm Follows the Storm

Father Lawrence C. Smith, S.J.
(Dhahran, Saudi Arabia)

I was deep in the Arabian desert staring out at the arid wasteland from my Humvee. The offensive was over, and we were heading toward home. I was meditating on the Resurrection and all the Easter week events when I was abruptly startled by something flying through the air toward me. Months of ministering to the troops of Operation Desert Storm had honed my natural sense of caution . . . that "thing" flying through the air might just be a deadly Scud missile.

But it wasn't. It was a butterfly. First one, then several of the beautiful insects.

It was a sign. A sign of new life in the desert. Easter in the desert wastes of Islam.

Then I heard birds chirping. A foreign sound in a strange and foreign land. A land of scorpions, heat, and snakes . . . of socially suppressed Arab women being defended by liberated (and liberating) American women in uniform. A land where the sacred chaplain's cross could not be displayed for fear of offending the local culture . . . and the Saudi desert sand was considered too sacred to be shoveled into sandbags for the defense of the nation.

Many confessions and conversions took place in this ancient desert during Desert Storm. I wondered what the Saudis would think of the Christian and Jewish witness that occurred in their holy desert. Their desert had been made holy thousands of years ago by Jewish tribes fleeing Egyptian slavery, hundreds of years ago by our Christian forefathers, and just weeks ago by young men coming forward to ask about becoming "an Army priest." Most important, we had made it holy with the blood of Americans left in the sands. We had made it holy once more.

And soon, through the flap of my Humvee, I noticed flowers and grass on the outskirts of Dhahran. Not having seen much of anything growing — except anxiety — for months in the desert, I began to understand that all was well. God was still with us in this alien land.

We'd survived Desert Storm. Now — by the grace of God — calm was returning to the desert after the storm. ☩

A 'Perfect' Fit

Father Joseph Scordo
(*Aboard the USS Saipan*)

After eighteen years in the priesthood, I was shocked at the letter I was reading from the military chief of chaplains. The chaplain shortage had become so serious, he said, that some segments of the Navy and Marine Corps could go as long as six months without religious services. Sufficiently surprised and saddened — but certain that I was too old — I phoned the recruiter mentioned in the letter.

The guy on the other end said, "How old are you?"

When I told him, he said, "Perfect."

Now there was no doubt. If forty-five was "perfect," the military was truly desperate. So, at an age when many officers retire, I joined the military.

It was in my small office aboard the USS Saipan that I realized just how critically important this job was. It was 1990, and we'd been sitting off the coast of Liberia for ninety blistering hot days waiting for possible orders to evacuate all noncombatants. Sitting aboard ship for three months, with little or no communication back home, can take its toll on sailors and Marines. It was getting to them, and I was there when they needed to unload.

"Being there" not only means giving the sacraments, it also means giving advice and support when things get rough. I'm the pipeline for Red Cross messages on board, some of which contain good news, and some not so good. On one occasion I had to tell a Marine that his brother had been killed in a shooting, and — because we were so late in getting the message — he was being buried that very day. On other occasions I'm happy to pass along a message that a sailor's wife had gotten the car transmission fixed, or that the bank had approved their mortgage application.

But I doubt that I've ever given advice that was as good as I got from a Navy chaplain just before I entered the service. Soon after that recruiter told me I was a "perfect" candidate, I began to have some second thoughts about joining. "If you're trying to escape authority, don't join," he said. "If you're trying to escape frustration, don't join. But if you really want to go to work for God, join."

That's turned out to be "perfect" advice. ✝

Tom

Monsignor Robert Spiegel
(Augsburg, Germany)

I was stationed in Augsburg, Germany, in the early 1980s when I met a recent convert to the Catholic faith. His name was Tom Parlette. He was in his mid-thirties, lived at home, and held a master's degree in religious education. Before his conversion to Catholicism, Tom was committed to Christ as a very active Protestant.

The U.S. Army was employing Tom as a director of religious education for the Augsburg military community, where he worked closely with a number of Catholic priests. In fact, it was the devotion of these chaplains that drew Tom to Catholicism. Tom had written to a friend of these priests, "These are men of real substance and deep faith, who love their Church. To them the Eucharist and other sacraments are of paramount importance and they would endure any hardship to make them available to soldiers and their families."

As time progressed, Tom's interest in Catholicism and priests matured to an even higher level. Now he began to ponder the priesthood himself, and we discussed this new discernment for many hours into the night.

At this writing I am happy to identify Tom as Father Tom Parlette, a wonderful priest who now serves in my home diocese of Davenport, Tennessee. ✠

Climb Every Mountain

Father Robert Bruno, O.F.M.
(Dubrovnik, Croatia)

We were just landing in an Air Force transport that had been hit by lightning, and none of the passengers felt better for the experience.

Now a combat-ready MH-53 helicopter stood on the tarmac at Brindisi, Italy, with its engines running, waiting to take us across the Adriatic Sea to Dubrovnik. Minutes after leaving Italian airspace the crew tested its machine guns and defensive flare system. No one was taking any chances. And not one of us had a chance to catch our breath.

Our Critical Incident Stress Debriefing crew was keenly aware that travel plans had been cobbled together at the last minute. An Air Force 737 passenger plane had crashed into a Croatian mountainside, killing all thirty-six aboard. Our crew had been specially trained to provide direct psychological and spiritual assistance to the emotionally stressed rescue team. The fact that one of the passenger fatalities was U.S. Secretary of Commerce Ron Brown added high-level pressure and visibility to the scenario.

It was Good Friday, 1996, when three Army helicopters flew our team to within a mile of the Mountain of St. John the Baptist, where the carnage lay. We'd been directed by the White House to get the bodies off the mountain and back to the States by Easter. We couldn't realize until we trekked up there that there were no bodies to take off the mountain; there were only charred body parts, shredded luggage, and pathetic personal effects. A wallet here . . . a photo there . . . and the smell of death and diesel everywhere.

The joint forces of Croatia and the U.S. Army, Navy, Marines, and Air Force took significant risks and worked masterfully to get the job done. I kept an eye on everyone, especially the young medical personnel working their first turn in the morgue operation. They were struggling, but they hung in there.

When Holy Saturday morning dawned, we awoke to find two huge new airplanes on the runway, which formed the backdrop for a very moving departure service with the Archbishop of

Dubrovnik officiating. As the caskets were marched toward the planes in heartbreaking solemnity, I couldn't help notice that they were Air Force C-17 Airlifters.

Thank God they didn't send a 737. I doubt that I could ever again look at that plane without tears in my eyes. ✟

Archbishop Edwin F. O'Brien of the Archdiocese of the Military Services, USA, presents a specially prepared copy of *Blessings from the Battlefield* to Pope John Paul II in Rome on November 19, 2000.